CW00841441

The Lockdown Poems

Volume Two

For six-to-eleven-year-olds
of all ages

by Tully Potter

Hello!

The poems

UNLIKE most of the poems in the first volume, these were not written during the Lockdown – even though one is about Cyrus the Virus – but they had the same purpose, to entertain my grand-daughters Anaiya Nadarajah, aged eleven, and Laila Nadarajah, aged ten. I hope adults will enjoy them as well.

The Song of Og and The Ballad of a Fly were both written some time ago, although they have since been improved. I don't apologise for including two poems about flies, because they badly need champions. The Abdominable Snowman came about because I heard someone say abdominable instead of abominable on TV and it seemed too good to waste.

Clever Clara began with a true story and so did Grandpa and the Ketchup, but they have been much embroidered.

The idea of the Hooperpottermus goes back to the early 1960s, when I was on a journalism course with colleagues named Hooper and Erasmus, but the poem is new. Cecil the Snail, Hugh Hedgehog and Daisy the Cat made appearances in the first volume but wanted to be in this one too, and I was too soft-hearted to exclude them.

Illustrations and decorations are by Anaiya Nadarajah (front cover, pages 14, 22 & 27), Laila Nadarajah (pages 36, 45, 49, 52, 54, 57 & 68), Sophie Nathan (pages 61 & 73), Richard Burch (pages 11, 17, 24, 29, 43, 58, 64, 66, 71 & 72), Emma Crawford (page 4), George Crawford (page 8), Jackson Day (page 16), Esmie and Harrison Crawford (page 32) and Haro Hodson (back cover).

Many thanks, as before, to Patrick Powell of St Breward Press, Cornwall, who designed the book, put it all together, made helpful suggestions and dealt patiently with my nervous twitchings.

GRANDPA AND THE KETCHUP

For Laila

The fish and chip supper was going quite well,
The church warden was thinking of buying a
    new bell;
A successful fund-raiser looked like a real cert
Until Grandpa let fly with his great
    ketchup squirt.

He thought he was aiming quite well at
    the fish
But the red stream completely missed
    the dish;
He tried squeezing as strongly as he was able
And another huge pool appeared on the table.

Then he gave a really tremendous squeeze
And hit Mrs McGinty right on the knees;
Tomato ketchup flew here and flew there
And some even got in the vicar's white hair.

It spurted and squirted in every direction,

Giving several people a bright red complexion;
But though it gushed out with a
  frightening force,
Granny's fish and chip supper remained free
  of sauce.

'Now dear,' Granny said, 'try just once more
  with feeling!'
But the next jet of ketchup shot up at
  the ceiling;
Parishioners dived in sheer fear of their lives
And brave husbands tried to shield
  terrified wives.

That ketchup container was like a wild thing
As it sprayed scarlet sauce with a splat! and
  a ping!
Three men might have brought it back
  under control
But no one would touch it with a barge-pole.

By the time Grandpa managed to get his
  aim straight,
All the chips had been joggled off poor
  Granny's plate;

'At last,' he exclaimed, 'I have got this
 thing beaten!'
But the bottle was empty, the fish had
 been eaten.

THE GREEN JELLY

Friends, it wasn't a ring and it wasn't a knock,
It was something quite flabby, just like a
  wet sock;
When we opened the door we could see this
  green shlock
Which wobbled and bobbled and oozed –
  what a shock!

It squelched through the door, slinking
  straight up the stairs,
It was like those vile things that you see
  in nightmares;
It tried out all the beds and then turned to
  the chairs,
Just like Goldilocks testing the home of
  three bears.

Then it squeezed through a window, slid down
  the roof ridge,
Headed straight for the kitchen, squashed up
  like a squidge,
And in no time at all it had opened
  the fridge,

Where it sampled each dish by absorbing
    a smidge.

I never met anything quite so bright green!
It glowed like a night-light and shone
    with a sheen;
It was much more revolting than anything
    I'd seen
And something about it seemed mucky
    and mean.

It turned on the hi-fi and shimmied
    and shivered,
It watched children's TV and quavered
    and quivered;
It sat at the keyboard and tickled the keys,
It meddled with mobiles and played with PCs.

It went into the garden and stayed there
    for hours
As it slithered and slid over grass, trees
    and flowers;
Even bad weather didn't diminish its powers,
For it gleamed even greener through
    downpours and showers.

It shuddered through mud and it rippled
through rain,
Then the day brightened up and it trembled
in vain;
It just melted in sunshine and ran down
a drain
And thank goodness that jelly was not
seen again.

HUGH HEDGEHOG

So how do you do? I'm a hedgehog
   named Hugh,
I'm the one with a back full of prickles;
I have my own fleas from my nose to my knees
And when they start biting, it tickles.

It helps to have bristles when traipsing
   through thistles,
I really enjoy being prickly;
If I'm frightened at all, I curl into a ball
And when danger's gone, I can move quickly.

If you want to leave food, I don't want to
   be rude
But milk is not what hedgehogs like;
A tin of cat's meat will go down a treat,
I can share it out with my mate Spike.

If you build me a house, I'll stay quiet as
   a mouse,
Just make sure I have plenty of bedding;
When the snow gets too deep, I go into a sleep
And I wake up when spring's really spreading.

It's not much expense to cut a hole in
  your fence
So hedgehogs can go to and fro;
Just four inches square will answer
  our prayer
And we'll all help your garden to grow.

 If it creeps, if it crawls,
  if it likes to
  climb walls,
We shall eat it with
  pleasure and zest;
The beetles we munch
make a marvellous crunch
And we lunch out on any old pest.

We'll sleep under a mix of old wood and
  dry sticks
But one thing you have to remember:
When you light a bonfire, don't make
  it a pyre
And roast us on Fifth of November.

Ponds are all very well, wells are all very well,
But how does a hedgehog get out?

I know I can swim but if I can't reach
    the brim,
I'm done for, however I shout.
Our five hoglets are blind but they don't
    really mind,
Spike makes sure that they're warm and
    well fed;
With their spines soft and white they could
    give you a fright
So we keep them confined to our bed.

In no time at all they'll
    look like us,
    though small,
With their eyes
    twinkling like
    little pins;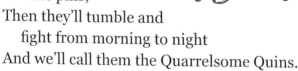
Then they'll tumble and
    fight from morning to night
And we'll call them the Quarrelsome Quins.

When it's just after dark in your garden
    or park
And the fox ventures out from his hole,
You may hear a huffle or even a snuffle:
Then you'll know Hugh's on flowerbed patrol.

THE TAIL OF KIT KANGAROO

For Anaiya

Kit Kangaroo carried her young in a pouch
And each time she jumped, she would holler
 out: 'Ouch!
'My poor feet are constantly giving me gyp
'And my poor old tail aches from its root
 to its tip.

'My family all think that I ought to be lollopy
'And dash round the Outback just like a young
 wallaby;
'In a zoo I would have my own personal vet
'And be cared for all day, like my dear Auntie
 Bet.

'The tourists expect me to carry my Joey
'But between you and me, he's all heely
 and toey;
'It isn't much fun when you're out for a run
'And your pouch is being punctured or
 punched by your son.'

So she sought the advice of a cunning
    old Wombat
Whose ears had been bitten and battered
    in combat;
'How on earth can I put the spring back
    in my leaps
'And make sure that I don't keep collapsing
    in heaps?'

Wombat said: 'For a cure you don't have
    to go far,
'What you need is a weekend of rest at
    the Spa;
'They'll trim all your toenails and then groom
    your fur
'And let you lie down, so you don't have to stir.

'They'll give you a massage and dose you
    with jollop
'And you'll leave on the Monday all ready
    to lollop.'
'But who's going to look after Joey for me?
'He's used to me giving him lunch, milk
    and tea!'

'No problems,' said Wombat. 'Their
    trained Cassowary
'Can go and fetch Joey fresh milk from
    the dairy;
'It's just the right place for a groucher
    or oucher
'And here is a ten-dollars-off special voucher.'

Then clutching her voucher, Kit loped to
    the Spa
Where the staff made her welcome, just like a
    film star;
They primped her and preened her and
    manicured each paw
And massaged her tail where she said it
    felt sore.

Now Kit bounds around like a new kangaroo
And never complains that she's feeling
    quite blue;
She returns to the Spa for her regular stints
And hosts a popular podcast about
    beauty hints.

OH DAISY!

For Anaiya

Oh Daisy!
Why do you sit in the middle of the door
Or even worse, right in the corridor?
And as we're stepping over you, why insist
On moving, so that our legs get in a twist?
Oh Daisy!

Oh Daisy!
Why do you wake up at three in the morning
And tear round the house without
    any warning?
Why do you want to go out in the rain
So we have to wait to let you in again?
Oh Daisy!

Oh Daisy!
Why do you turn up your nose at your food
When we know the pouches we give you are good?
And why do you sit on all of the chairs
So our best clothes get furred with white hairs?
Oh Daisy!

Oh Daisy!
Why expose your belly with paws in the air
Then grab us with claws when we stroke
    you there?
And why, when you're sitting so quiet in my lap,
Stick those same claws in till I look like a map?
Oh Daisy!

Oh Daisy!
Why do all your strange feline feelings quicken
As soon as I open the bag with our chicken?
And how, before I can even start carving,
Do you appear, meowing as if you are starving?
Oh Daisy!

PLOD THE DIPLODOCUS

I'm known as Diplodocus, 'Plod' if you like,
The earth really shakes when I go on a hike;
I have a small head on a very long neck
And before I move anything, I have to check.

Many metres of me join my uppermost lip
To the end of my long tail, the tippermost tip;
And sending out messages puts quite a strain
On a big dinosaur with a peanut-sized brain.

Standing on my hind legs, with my tail
    as a prop,
I can reach all the leaves in the tasty treetop;
But if I want to burp, it must really be strong
To get into my throat and then travel along.

In my spare time I quite like to strum a guitar,
Which is hard when your paws are as big as
    mine are;
I'm likely to tread on guitars that I've played
And their squashed wrecks are scattered all
    over the glade.

We weigh twenty tons each, and nobody can
    floor us,
Although there's a cheeky young chap,
    Allosaurus,
Who thinks he
    can creep
    up, without
    saying 'Allo,
And take a big
    bite – he's
    so quick,
    we're
    so slow.

But I can still
    fetch him
    a jolly
    good clip
With my
    eighty-bone
    tail, which I use
    like a whip;
So most of the time I can spend all my days
Just strumming and humming and having
    a graze.

RUNNY HONEY MANGO TANGO

For Laila

If your honey's far too runny
It will go just everywhere;
When the day is hot and sunny
You will find it in your hair.

So if I had lots of money
And my hands were not so licky,
I'd ask bees for pots of honey
That would never make me sticky.

For their Queen I'd make a beeline
And take Daisy Cat to her,
Saying: 'O Queen, pity this feline
Who has honey in her fur.

'What we want is all the sweetness
'That we find so very yummy;
'But we find we lose our neatness
'When our hair or fur is gummy.'

. . . .

If you tango with a mango
You must watch out for the juice
Which will trickle down your trousers
And make puddles in your shoes.

If you want to eat a mango
You should climb into a bath
So the juice will wash straight off you,
It's the recommended path.

. . . .

Eating chicken from Kentucky
May be finger-lickin' good;
But unless you're very lucky
It's an elbow-lickin' food.

I like chicken-in-a-basket
But the fat runs through the cracks;
So I keep it in a casket
And I seal it up with wax.

. . . .

If you eat a watermelon
You can have a nice cool wash,
But please keep your wellies well on
Or your feet will get a splosh.

All these foods we like for dinner
Help us frolic, skip and frisk;
And we'd be a whole lot thinner
If we didn't take the risk.

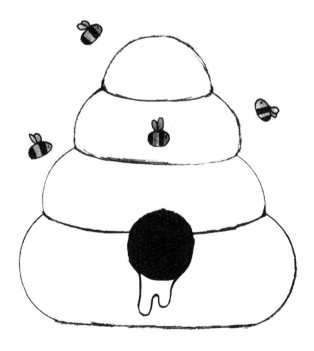

THE SONG OF OG

Og, King of Bashan was a good eight
   cubits high;*
Though Gog was large, and Magog huge,
To him they were small fry.

His bed was a full nine cubits long
And at least four cubits wide;
It had a massive frame of iron
With two great iron legs each side.

His clogs were made from the skin of a hog,
He drank from a four-gallon firkin of grog
And went for a jog with a six-foot-tall dog.

I can't think of anyone quite like old Og
Though I know of the travels of Phileas Fogg
And the cat-astrophic adventures of Mogg.

There was Pippity Pog
Who wrote a long blog
Which everyone found a dreadful slog;
There was long King Log
Who lounged in a bog

And disappointed every frog;
There was Noggin the Nog
From the Nordic iced fog
Whose exploits had all the children agog;
And King Zog of Albania was terribly,
 terribly tall
But Og, King of Bashan was the biggest of
 them all.

*As a Biblical character, Og used a
Biblical measurement – a cubit equals
almost half a metre.*

THE TEARFUL BUT TUNEFUL TIZWOZ

The Tizwoz lives just up the creek
He doesn't grunt, he doesn't speak
But now and then the tears will seep
Out of his eyes when half asleep.

It's no good asking what is wrong;
He'll only burst into a sad song
Which sounds like Greek to you and me,
Though Greeks don't seem to have the key.

I can't think what he sings about,
I wish he'd scream or shriek or shout
But on and on he drones and wails;
I'm sure he's telling frightful tales.

Perhaps he met a rude baboon
Who burst his red-and-blue balloon;
Perhaps a rather clumsy fawn
Trod right upon his painful corn.

Perhaps a duck-billed platypus
Pulled all his long tail-feathers loose;

Perhaps a very spiteful cat
Threw cowpats at him with a splat.

Perhaps ... but no, we'll never know
What makes the Tizwoz warble so;
One time, I thought I'd found the cause,
I made him cease his song and pause.

Just as his chant was in full flow,
I joined him in his dirge of woe;
He seemed to love it – for a while
It looked as if he'd almost smile.

But then I realised I was wrong:
He launched into a wilder song
And, worried that he'd burst my ears,
I left him to his tuneful tears.

The Tizwoz lives just up the creek;
He doesn't sneeze, he doesn't squeak,
But tears keep rolling down his cheek;
I'm sure his life can't be too bad,
I don't think he's completely mad,
I feel he quite likes being sad.

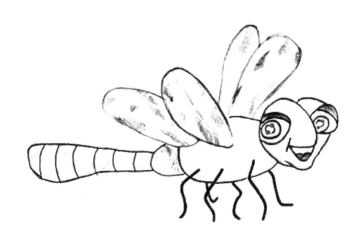

How do you like
the poems so far?

THE TERRIBLE TWO AT THE TIP

For Laila

The house was in such an appalling
    deep clutter,
With unwanted things almost stacked to
    the gutter,
That Mummy announced they would go to
    the tip
And Tallulah and Tara could come for
    the trip.

So they filled up the car with a fine load of tat
Like a TV, a kettle, two pans and a mat,
Six bottles, a cracked plate, a broken toy truck,
A shredder, a chair seat, all kinds of old muck.

Then off to the big council tip Mummy drove
With the girls quite hemmed in by this strange
    treasure trove.
'Now stay in the car,' she said as they went in;
'We don't want you two mixed with plastic
    and tin.'

But Tara, who hated being out of
    the action,
Found the great bins of rubbish a
    fateful attraction;
She sneaked up some steps when no one
    was about,
Fell off into a bin and clean knocked
    herself out.

A man who liked searching the tip for
    cheap loot
Picked her up with some wood, stowed her
    into his boot
And drove away, thinking: 'That is a
    nice model;
'I can make something good, it'll just be
    a doddle.'

When Tallulah told Mummy of this
    latest antic
The two of them looked for the tip-man,
    quite frantic.
'Well ma'am,' said the tip-man, 'that sounds
    like old Bob;
'He always needs stuff for some recycling job.

'But he's rather short-sighted and takes some
    weird stuff
'And if I try to help, he gets into a huff;
'You'll find that his shack is just down
    by the lake
'And you'll smell the nice food that his wife
    likes to bake.'

So Mum and Tallulah drove down to the water
And Mummy said: 'Bob, have you taken
    my daughter?'
'Oh yes,' old Bob answered. 'I do beg
    your pardon.
'I thought she was a statue to put in
    the garden.

'I have a confession – don't fuss, shout
    or stamp:
'I've already recycled her into a lamp;
'I've just fitted a nice LED bulb from Louth
'And it lights up quite well, coming out
    of her mouth.'

'I'm speechless!' said Mummy, which wasn't
    quite true,

As she said lots of things and the air was
    quite blue;
But meanwhile Tallulah, the girl of the hour,
Crept out into the kitchen and turned off
    the power.

She soon released Tara, undoing the clamp
That made her look just like a little girl lamp;
And the two of them, followed by Mummy,
    rushed out,
Tumbled into the car and went home.
    'Without doubt,'

Mummy said, 'girls, that's the very last time
'That we go to the tip; Tara does like to climb
'But I think that in future, we'll visit a glen;
'And we'll put out our trash for the rag-and-
    bone men.'

THE WYSIWYG*

For Laila

The Wysiwyg, the Wysiwyg,
Is nothing like a guinea pig;
He isn't small, he isn't big,
He'll balance on a hazel twig.

What You See Is What You Get
The mother tells her brood;
But when she isn't looking
He'll do something really rude.

The Wysiwyg, the Wysiwyg,
Is such a silly tizzy tig,
He'll grab a jar and take a swig,
Then dance a jolly jazzy jig.

Be kind to Wysiwygs, my dears:
Their visits are quite rare;
You wouldn't want to scream or shout
And give them all a scare.

The Wysiwyg, the Wysiwyg,
Will take you on a dizzy dig
To find a funny thingamajig
That's fallen off a whirligig.

If a Wysiwyg comes visiting
Be sure to give him tea;
But go easy with the fruit cake
As he'll eat enough for three.

The Wysiwyg, the Wysiwyg,
He doesn't care a fizzy fig!
He likes to wear a lilac sprig
And dress himself in fancy rig.

That's all I know of the Wysiwyg!

The clue is in the fifth line.

THE THOUGHTFUL SLOTH

For Anaiya

The sloth was philosophical:
While hanging upside down,
He took to thinking about life
With a concentrated frown.

'Am I a sloth who rhymes with cloth
'Or a sloath who rhymes with loath?'
And he came to the conclusion
That he was a bit of both.

'Do I have three toes or only two?
'I've never thought to look.
'Three toes would be much easier
'If I want to read a book.

'My fur grows mostly wrong way round
'And teems with lice and moths.
'Do I have to eat just leaves and stalks?
'I must ask some other sloths.'

Such questions did not trouble him
For more than half an hour;
On a sunny day he liked to snooze,
If it rained he took a shower.

He swayed a little in the breeze
As he dangled from his branch,
And thought: 'To make me budge from here
'Would take an avalanche.'

If you see a sloth just hanging around
Within the undergrowth,
Take the time to ask him: 'Do I, sir,
'Address a Sloth or Sloath?'

And if you want to be polite,
Be sure to doff your hat
But do it slo-o-o-wly, upside down;
He'll be tickled pink by that.

THE UNLOVED ONION

An onion girl moped in a vegetable bed
And pulled the brown earth up over her head;
'Oh, nobody loves me at all,' she said,
'Even though I'm beautifully round and red.

'I've been sitting out here for what seems
    like years,
'Waiting until a boyfriend appears;
'But the Brussels sprouts and
    asparagus spears
'Take one sniff at me and burst into tears.

'My mother thought I would be quite a catch
'For any young sprig in the vegetable patch,
'And any sensible suitor would snatch
'At the chance to make such an
    excellent match.

'I thought I had a bouquet just like roses
'But carrots parade past and wrinkle
    their noses;
'They threaten to take me and wash me
    with hoses,

'Which makes me sadder than
   anyone supposes.'

She did her utmost to attract some cool guys
And puffed herself up to a gigantic size;
But all the potatoes shielded their eyes
And said they would rather be made into fries.

Then one day she spied a healthy young leek
Who was tall and handsome and slim
   and sleek;
'I've been looking for someone like you
   for a week,'
He said as his long green leaves brushed
   her cheek.

'I have to implore you: will you be mine?
'I think you're so round that you look
   quite divine
'And what I like best is, you smell
   so fine,
'Like a gorgeously delicate onion wine.'

'Can this be so?' the onion girl thought;
'He doesn't look like the deceiving sort.'

To the leek, she said, 'I'm quite overwrought,
'I feel I've been hit by a juggernaut!'

It was love at first sight between those two
But what became of them, I never knew;
Some say they both ended up in a stew,
Blending aromas as vegetables do;
I'm sure such a tragedy cannot be true
So the end of the story I'll leave up to you.

HOW FINE TO BE A FLY

How fine to be a flighty fly
Flitting to and fro,
Alighting on a pigsty
And then on Auntie Flo.

Some people when they spot us
Cover up their food;
They even try to swat us,
Which we think is rather rude.

We lay our eggs on old meat
Like beef or lamb or faggots;
Our babies don't get cold feet
Because they're legless maggots.

We like to buzz around you,
Especially at night;
It's no good saying 'Confound you!'
Or switching off the light.

Right in your ear we prickle
When you try to have a doze;

And our six legs really tickle
When we settle on your nose.

A lot of people wonder
Where we go when it gets cold;
We like to gather under
Any roof with nasty mould.

THE GREAT PASTRY SNATCH

I must tell you about the appalling to-do
When Tallulah and Tara, the Terrible Two,
Went down to the seaside with their
    faithful Mummy
And Tara complained: 'I've a quite
    empty tummy.'

She chose from the food stall a huge
    sausage roll
Which took one look at Tara and swallowed
    her whole!
'Oh dear!' Mummy said, 'Tara does overdo it...
'Remember the time she ate six pounds
    of suet?

'But this is the first time I've heard
    of a girl
'Being grabbed by her food and gulped
    down in a whirl.'
Yet worse was to follow: a vast Cornish pasty
Had clearly decided Tallulah looked tasty.

It opened itself like a giant scallop shell
And in no time Tallulah had vanished as well.
Then to Mummy's great horror, those two
    pastry brutes
Slithered down off the stall – they were in
    real cahoots.

While Mummy called 'Help! Police!' they slid
    to the quay,
Stole a boat and were soon heading right out
    to sea.
A police sergeant said: 'Madam, our force is
    no good.
'We need someone experienced in
    runaway food.'

The RAF scrambled at least fourteen eggs,
The Navy shipped snacks on asparagus legs,
An onion bargee dispatched bhajis by
    the score
And bands of samosas patrolled the seashore.

The Italians sent pizzas skimming over
    the waves,

Saying: 'Porca miseria! We must catch
   those knaves!'
The Germans launched boatfuls of
   pork and sauerkraut
And the Irish distributed barrels
   of stout.

The Ukrainians put pancakes in missiles
   and drones,
The Scots hurled a haggis and thousands
   of scones;
The Welsh offered Welsh cakes and cheese
   from Caerphilly,
The Swedes pumped out oat milk, which I
   think was silly.

Then, just as they'd led all these
   foodstuffs a dance,
The Terrible Two calmly landed in France;
'We got so terrifically hungry,' they cried,
'That we ate up those criminals from
   the inside.'

If there is a moral to this toothsome tale

It is: if you see mammoth pastries for sale,
Make sure, even if you believe they
   are yummy,
That your eyes aren't too big for the size of
   your tummy.

KEVIN THE KOALA

For Laila

There was a Koala called Kevin
Who liked to feel quite close to heaven;
So he sat up a gum-tree
Twice as tall as a plum-tree
And munched leaves from 6.00 to 11.00.

But a muscular logger, Big Bruce,
Who usually liked to fell spruce,
Thought: 'Spruce is so nondescript
'But a nice eucalypt
'I could put to a wide range of use.'

So he phoned his mate Steve, an odd-jobber
And said: 'I've a task for you, cobber,
'A massive great gum;
'Leave your barbie and come
'And bring all your lumberjack clobber.'

Then each took up his heaviest axe
And gave Kevin's old tree mighty whacks,

Till it started to sway
And I'm sorry to say
That Kevin was sick down their backs.

That made them redouble their force
Until Kevin was thrown off, of course;
'I'm just a marsupial,
'Not a bold loop-the-loopial!'
He wailed, flying into some gorse.

But a kind girl named Kerry came past
And saw Kevin's plight: 'I'm aghast!'
She said: 'You clumsy brutes
'With your axes and boots
'Have knocked this poor beast
    off his mast.'

Then she took Kevin back to her farm
And treated his bruises with balm;
Among sweet-smelling shrubs
He ate witchetty grubs,
Thinking: 'Here I can come to
    no harm.'

Today Kevin lives not far from Kerry

With two friends in a fine flowering cherry;
She brings them gum leaves
In thick bundles and sheaves
Which they chew with a cool glass of sherry.

CLEVER CLARA

The word went out on Maconachie's Farm:
'Clara the cow has come to some harm!
'She should be gently chewing the cud
'But she's in the lake and stuck in the mud!'

The cowherd Bert took his mobile phone
To dial 999, saying: 'I'm alone
'And here on the farm it's an emergency;
'We need a helicopter with urgency!'

Said the coastguard: 'We can't send
   out a chopper
'Unless the accident's a real whopper.'
'But our prize cow Clara is in the lake!
'We require some help and no mistake.'

The gallant men of the RNLI
Launched their D-class lifeboat to do or die;
They tried to tempt her out with some food
But Clara just wasn't in the mood.

Bert put a halter around her neck
But Clara seemed to moo: 'What the heck?

'I'm not going to move for any old rope.'
So after a while they gave up hope.

Two policemen, Constables Hill and O'Hara
Said: 'We hear you've got trouble with Clara;
'Why don't we all try to pull her out?
'We'll take the strain when you give
     us a shout.'

So they tugged and tugged with might
     and main
But Clara just mooed and slipped back again;
'I'm knackered,' Hill panted, 'we need
     an X-factor
'Like Farmer Maconachie with his tractor.'

The farmer said: 'Lads, I know
     something bigger;
'The garage man Pat has a gigantic digger.
'Let's go and see if he'll lend it to us
'And we'll hoick the cow out with no
     further fuss.'

Then off they all went, for the JCB
And Clara thought: 'That's bound to hurt me;

'I know I'm rather round in the figure
'But I really don't relish being grabbed
   by a digger.'

Instead of just going into a sulk
She made a great effort to move her bulk:
She got her front legs up on to the bank
And the back legs followed, with a fierce yank.

When the men came back with the
   huge machine,
Clever Clara was nowhere to be seen;
She had wandered off to have a quiet munch
On some clover she fancied for her lunch.

THE BALLAD OF A FLY

A fly went walking, one two three
Up and down my old TV;
It was a sight for you to see
My darling.

He ruined a Russian statesman's frown,
Explored a lady of renown
And added a jewel to her crown
My darling.

An old field-marshal's martial cry
Did not abash my gallant fly
Who neatly blacked-out his left eye
My darling.

In a very tense Cup Final match
One goal the goalie could not catch;
My fly's was best of all the batch
My darling.

Throughout the trendy pundits' talk
That insect had a pleasant walk;

Even when they sang he did not baulk
My darling.

He marched in a ceremonial scene,
Tickled a very reverend dean
And vanished when they played 'The Queen'
My darling.

ARISTOTLE

I

Aristotle found a bottle,
Took a hearty drink;
But Socrates was such a tease,
He'd filled it full of ink.

II

Has anyone seen my axolotl?
He answers to Hector Aristotle;
His body's a lovely brown-gold mottle,
But he'll die without his water bottle;
And I really can't imagine what'll
Happen to him – I hope he's not ill.

CECIL THE SNAIL

One day Cecil the snail crept into a pail
And suddenly felt a strange motion;
For he'd chosen the bucket of little
    Tom Tuckett
Who loved going down to the ocean.

They went in a car and it wasn't too far
Till they came to a long golden strand;
Cecil said: 'I'm a snail and I can't make a trail
'On this loose, gritty, shape-shifting sand.'

Pools left by the tide stretched out far
    and wide
With strange plants for small fish to shelter;
The sand might be coarse but he watched
    a seahorse
Driving tiny copepods helter-skelter.

Tommy ran to some rocks with mussels
    in flocks
And Cecil admired their dark shells;

Whelk shells had a twist, which was hard
   to resist,
And other shells could have been bells.

There were cockles like tents and winkles
   with dents
And a huge catfish in a white coat;
'That must be a doctor-puss and look! There's
   an octopus,'
Cried Cecil, 'and there's a lifeboat.'

He looked on as a hermit, without any permit,
Invaded a sea-snail's old house;
'That belonged to my cousin – fifteen to
   a dozen
'He'll think that old crab's a real louse!'

Another big pool was like going to school,
Cecil's eyes were right out on their stalks
When the cuttlefish cuttled, the velvet
   crabs scuttled
And did their sideways silly walks.

He saw starfish with suckers, periwinkles
  with puckers,

Anemones waving with joy,

Mottled blennies that blushed when naughty
  Tom rushed

To grab at prawns – just like a boy.

At the close of the day they drove out of
  the bay

And at home Cecil had a nice bin-doze:

'I'm so glad to be back where I'm safe
  from attack

'And can climb and slime over the windows.'

THE HOOPERPOTTERMUS

Of two fat men I'll tell the tale
Although the sensitive will quail
And some will say: 'Beyond the pale!'
Their days were spent down at the pub,
Or eating and drinking at their club
Until each one looked like a tub;
One was the would-be hunter Hooper
Who thought that he was rather super
But was inclined to make a blooper;
The other was my cousin Potter
Who liked the climate when 'twas hotter
But was the most offensive rotter.

To Africa they made their way,
With tents, guns, golf clubs and a sleigh,
Hoping to get rich in a day;
A Grand Safari was their plan
But trekking suited neither man
And when the summer rains began
They found they'd brought some silly gear;
'Woollies and scarves are no good here,'
Said Hooper, opening himself a beer,
'I need a proper rain-proof coat

'And this old sleigh will never float,
'We really should have brought a boat.'

'You're right,' said Potter, 'and the food
'We've brought with us is very crude;
'A round of golf will do us good.'
Out came the golf clubs, woods and irons,
But they and their caddies, Figg and Bryans,
Were ambushed by a pride of lions:
In vain Figg, Bryans and the porters
Tried to prevent the fearful slaughters
But there was blood upon the waters;
At last the lions were in retreat
When they had had enough to eat
But Hooper's heart had ceased to beat.

This woe was only to be feared,
As his top half had disappeared
And Potter had similarly been sheared;
There was, between him and his friend,
Only enough to make a blend
Of half a fat man at each end;
But who would do the operation
When they were far from civilisation?
The survivors frowned in deep frustration;

But then came, in the nick of time,
A doctor seeking a warmer clime
Who'd heard about the lions' crime.

The noted surgeon Sidney Snitch
Who specialised in snip and stitch
Said: 'It will go without a hitch
'If we can find enough tough thread
'Before both men are really dead;
'Let's hoist them up on to their sled.'
He worked all day, with Nurse Liz Truss,
And thus was born, without much fuss,
The dreaded Hooperpottermus,
Which can be seen, rolling and dipping
In Africa's rivers, sliding, slipping,
A danger to bathers, beasts and shipping.

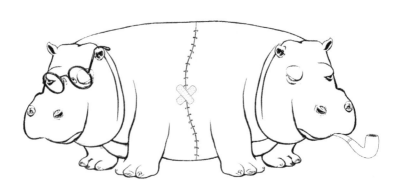

CYRUS THE VIRUS

Cyrus the Virus was ghastly to see
With twenty-two legs and five eyes;
He had horrid moist mouths, at least
    seventy-three,
Fit to frighten the spiders and flies.

Cyrus loved to spread fevers and
    other diseases
Like measles, rubella and mumps;
He thought it was funny to hear coughs
    or sneezes
And see people down in the dumps.

He didn't think much of a mere common cold
But rejoiced when folk came out in spots;
The redder the better, and quite uncontrolled,
So they looked like a great mass of dots.

He would often be seen round downtown
    rubbish bins
With his pet flu germ Warty in tow;
While Cyrus would look in the discarded tins
Eating dog poo made Warty just glow.

They laughed when the humans got out
    a huge spray
And squirted it east, west, north, south;
For Cyrus would say, 'I could eat that all day'
As he rolled it around his best mouth.

'They kill ninety-nine-point-nine percent of
    the germs
'But Warty's the other point-one;
'Sprays don't even bother the woodlice
    and worms,
'In fact they just add to our fun.'

When Cyrus grew old, it was time to retire
To Long Covid, a nice Cotswold village
With a fine refuse heap, full of muck, mess
    and mire,
And for Warty, some really vile spillage.

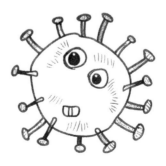

THE ABDOMINABLE SNOWMAN

I made a snowman, tall and white,
With eyes of pebbles, shining bright;
He had a carrot for his nose
And old black shoes instead of toes.

A slice of melon formed his mouth,
Red buttons ran from north to south;
He wore a rather battered hat,
His coat was tight – he was too fat.

He stood there, looking fine and proud,
But oh! his rumbles were so loud!
Inside his frame, his sounds abdominal
Were deafening – they were phenomenal.

He burbled on through day and night,
His gurgles gave the cat a fright;
It seemed the noise would never cease,
I thought someone would call the police.

One day we had a dreadful storm
And then the weather grew quite warm;
At first the snowman matched the thunder
But then he weakened – and no wonder.

The sun was causing him to melt!
His coat fell off, his hat of felt
Slipped down into a crazy angle;
His twiggy arms were in a tangle.

I watched as his once-mighty rumble
Diminished to a sort of grumble;
Then it became a low, sad mumble,
His eyes, mouth, nose all took a tumble.

His shoes and buttons lay in mush
For he was dwindling in a rush;
My snowman, once so clean and cool,
Soon turned into a muddy pool.

THE AARDVARK ROMANCE

A lone aardvark lived out on the African plain
And he wished that he had just a little
    more brain;
He pondered and pondered and wondered
    and wondered
And tried to think where in his life he
    had blundered.

'I have a hard problem I cannot work out,'
He sighed as he hoovered ants up through
    his snout;
'I would love to keep house with a nice
    aardvark mate,
'But I fear I have left it a little too late.

'At the edges my long ears are starting
    to crinkle,
'My skin, which was smooth, is beginning
    to wrinkle,
'My eyesight, once keen, is in need of
    some checks
'But who ever heard of an aardvark
    with specs?'

He had a nice burrow to keep cool all day
And he came out at dusk to pursue
  insect prey;
'Two is company when you are trying
  to forage,
'A fine female could help me and stir the
  ant-porridge.'

Then he had an idea – 'I could try advertising;
'There must be a website for aardvark-
  advising.'
So he got out his laptop and soon went online
To see if he could find the right partner
  to dine.

'A gentleman aardvark is seeking a date
'With a lady who's not yet discovered
  her mate.'
That was what he put up on the
  Aardvark Website,
Then he went out and hunted for termites
  all night.

What joy! Next day came a reply from a widow

Who went by the name of Miss
 Gwendolen Prideaux;
Her poor husband had met the
 unfortunate fate
Of being eaten by lions when he stayed
 out too late.

She had grown tired of ploughing her own
 lonely furrow
And quite fancied the notion of sharing
 his burrow;
Their May wedding attracted a vast
 aardvark throng
And the Massed Warthog Choirs entertained
 with a song.

JUST LIKE A RAT

I planned a long poem about a rat
But he ate all my paper, so that is that;
I might have forgiven him, there and then,
If he hadn't also chewed up my pen.

He even ate his
picture and
the frame!

RAT

Goodbye!

Printed in Great Britain
by Amazon

40698788R00046